# The Little Church Bird

by Phyllis Didleau

Illustrated by Gretchen Gackstatter

The Little Church Bird
First edition, August 1, 2021
Original illustrations in watercolor by Gretchen Gackstatter

Published by BOOK BOOK SQUARED
P.O. Box 60144
Colorado Springs, Colorado 80960

Printed in the United States of America

ISBN 978-1-943829-39-2

**www.goldenrulemasterpieces.com**
**www.mangermouse.com**

BOOK BOOK SQUARED is an imprint of Rhyolite Press, LLC

**BOOK BOOK²**

Once upon a time in the space above us called the sky, God's voice was heard.

"My goodness," He exclaimed, "the expanse of this area is larger than I had imagined. I was sure My blueprints were read and carried out according to My instructions. I remember speaking this into existence, but I didn't think it was so vast."

"Let's see. How can I correct this?" God sat upon His heavenly throne and pondered the answer to His own question. "Shrink it, perhaps. No, I can't do that. Why, it already reaches from the beginning to the end. That would be such a job that even I wouldn't want to tackle it.

Scrap it and start over? Ouch!

That would be going back on My word. I can't do that . . ."

"Embellish it? Hey, now that isn't such a bad idea. Let's see, with what could I embellish it? Music? Maybe. But what could I use as a source? Objects of creation?
But what would I create to fill such an expanse as this?"

"Aha! Whatever I create would have to be able to dodge snowflakes, stay out of the rain, move from place to place easily and also be able to seek after its own food. By Jove, I think I am on to something! In order to fill the space, it must be able to fly, yet settle down on the earth to find food for itself and young ones."

"And I will even place within each one of them a song. A song! Oh, what a great idea! The sky will be filled with fowl of the air that will enhance the heavenly sanctuary! Oh, I am so excited. I am getting a great Godly idea! I'll make a little fowl of the air that will come in different sizes and different colors! Oh, how beautiful they will be!"

I SING BECAUSE IM HAPPY.
I SING BECAUSE IM FREE.
HIS EYE IS ON THE SPARROW.
AND I KNOW HE WATCHES ME.

"Their song will be a joy to all who arise especially early to hear the trills and whistles. All day long they will sing to the earth and all that is on it. Well, I must get busy. I have so much to do."

God returned to His planning and operations room and pulled
His office throne up to His drawing board. He pulled some
colors from the rainbow and set about mixing
some new shades.
He tuned in to the sounds of the wind and waters
and began to blend octaves, flats, and sharps.

For the covering on the fowl, He took whisps of His own hair and wove them along with fine clover and weeds and developed a whole new apparel He called a feather. Then, the body He made of fine, hollow stems He took from the angels' garden. It was so light it needed only a slight up and down movement of the appendages on each side to get it airborne. Because He took it from the angels' garden He called the appendages, as He had called the angel's appendages, wings. Once upon the wing, so to speak, the fowl could catch the currents of the air to take it great distances.

"Wow," God excitedly whispered. "It's almost finished.
Won't all the earth creatures just love this!
I'll run into the new product development sanctuary
and get this in to production."
The fowl of the air started off the assembly line.
Angels were as excited as God Himself was!
"Oh, such color! Oh, just listen to the songs!"

"Oh, wait one heavenly moment! Stop production for a micro second. I must plant within each little fowl the ability to go South, North, East and West. I must plant within each a sense of direction so they will mysteriously be able to move with the seasons."

"I will give each one a mini-gram of My wisdom. They will have such instinct that all mankind will marvel and see a bit of the creator in them. Oh, what a mystery and joy they will be!"

God spoke and production began and continued until the heavens were full of color and song, filling the expanse He had been so concerned about.

It was late in the evening and God was headed for a good night's sleep after a busy day with the creation of the fowl. He just started to drift off, pulling the warmth of the sun up around Him when another idea caused Him to sit up, squint into the light of the moon and ponder still further on the fowl. He was so satisfied, yet He felt there was a measure yet to be completed. "I really don't like calling them all fowl," He thought as He gazed at the big dipper.

"I need another word. Another word...that's it! It will rhyme with word. A reminder that the spoken word brought it into being! Word...word...let's see...oh, I know! Bird, bird! That's it! Bird. How perfect. It rhymes with word! But one more thing! Every bird will have a special calling. Each song will reach the ear of the one it was created to reach. It will have a special place to build its nest. It will be seen by all who come to worship Me because it will be at the door of every house of Mine. It will call creation to come to the house of God. I will call it the Little Church Bird. Shhhh. Can you hear it? Can you hear the Little Church Bird?"

THE END

## Lessons from The Little Church Bird

God created the birds — Genesis 1:21

God created you — Jeremiah 1:1

God created all of us — Genesis 1:27

He has a special plan for you — Jeremiah 29:11

He has placed a gift within each one of us — James 1:17

We are expected to use the gift He has given us — James 1:22

Our gift is for a special purpose — 1 Timothy 4:14

Our gifts are to glorify God — Ephesians 4:12

The author, Phyllis Constant Didleau, holds a Bachelor Degree with a Life Certificate in elementary education from the University of Northern Colorado in Greeley. As a postgraduate student, she studied in Special Education at the University of Hawaii in Honolulu. Phyllis has many years experience in the classroom.

As a high school student she taught Sunday School and has been the Director of Children's Church. She has provided years of volunteering teaching children and participating in Vacation Bible School. Her Biblical studies include a two-year course from the Institute of Theology by Extension through the Department of International Studies, Open Bible Churches.

Gretchen Gackstatter, the illustrator, received a Bachelor Degree in Fine Arts from the University of Northern Colorado, Greeley. Over the years, she has taught art from kindergarten through high school. At the present time she teaches watercolor at the Argonne Gallery in St. Louis, Missouri. Her watercolors have gained a wide, popular reputation.